21st Century Junior Library

DISABILITY ETIQUETTE

Nicole Evans

easterseals

Understanding Disability

Published in the United States of America by:

Cherry Lake Press

2395 South Huron Parkway, Suite 200, Ann Arbor, Michigan 48104
www.cherrylakepress.com

Reading Adviser: Beth Walker Gambro, MS, Ed., Reading Consultant, Yorkville, IL

Photo Credits: © wavebreakmedia/Shutterstock.com, cover, 1; © Doro Guzenda/Shutterstock.com, 5; © WETSTOCK PRODUCTIONS/Shutterstock.com, 6; © Anna Kraynova/Shutterstock.com, 7; © Blue Titan/ Shutterstock.com, 8, 9; © jittawit21/Shutterstock.com, 10; © LightField Studios/Shutterstock.com, 11; © AnnGaysorn/Shutterstock.com, 12; © Jaren Jai Wicklund/Shutterstock.com, 14; © Denis Kuvaev/ Shutterstock.com, 17; © worawit_j/Shutterstock.com, 18; © Astafjeva/Shutterstock.com, 21

Cherry Lake Press is an imprint of Cherry Lake Publishing Group.

Library of Congress Cataloging-in-Publication Data
Names: Evans, Nicole (Nicole Lynn), author.
Title: Disability etiquette / by Nicole Evans.
Description: Ann Arbor, Michigan : Cherry Lake Publishing, [2022] | Series: Understanding disability | Includes bibliographical references. | Audience: Grades 2-3
Identifiers: LCCN 2022005412 | ISBN 9781668910702 (paperback) | ISBN 9781668909102 (hardcover) | ISBN 9781668912294 (ebook) | ISBN 9781668913888 (pdf)
Subjects: LCSH: People with disabilities—Juvenile literature. | Disabilities—Juvenile literature. | Etiquette—Juvenile literature.
Classification: LCC HV1568 .E9356 2022 | DDC 362.4—dc23/eng/20220214
LC record available at https://lccn.loc.gov/2022005412

Cherry Lake Press would like to acknowledge the work of the Partnership for 21st Century Learning, a Network of Battelle for Kids. Please visit http://www.battelleforkids.org/networks/p21 for more information.

Printed in the United States of America
Corporate Graphics

Easterseals is enriching education through greater disability equity, inclusion and access. Join us at www.Easterseals.com.

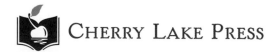

CONTENTS

WHAT IS DISABILITY?

The Americans with Disabilities Act (ADA) defines disability as "a physical or mental impairment that substantially limits one or more major life activities."

OMG! That is me! My name is Nicole Evans. I am a writer, actress, and disability **activist**. I am also a person with a disability. My disability is **osteogenesis imperfecta**. It is a bone condition that causes fragile bones and affects my ability to walk. I use a **manual** wheelchair to help me

People with disabilities make up a large portion of the population!

5

go from place to place and to keep me safe. My disability is just one of countless other types of disabilities that exist.

For example, there are visible disabilities and invisible disabilities. My disability is a visible disability because you can see my wheelchair and that I have a challenging time moving my legs. Other types of visible disabilities include cerebral palsy, muscular dystrophy, and dwarfism.

There are many different types of disabilities that affect children as well as adults.

Think!

Do you or someone you know have a disability? Is it a visible disability or an invisible disability?

An invisible disability is a disability that you cannot see, such as autism, diabetes, or ADHD.

Did you know that more than 61 million Americans have some type of disability? That is a large number! On average, that means one out of every four people has a disability. That makes the disabled community the largest **minority** group in the United States.

FOCUS ON THE PERSON

The most important thing to remember is that people with disabilities are just like everyone else. We have families, friends, homework, responsibilities, successes, and struggles.

Have you ever heard the phrase: *treat others how you want to be treated*? This wise rule applies to anyone that you interact with, including the disabled community.

Create!

How do you want to be treated? How should you treat others? Make a list! Be sure to include the words *kindness* and *respect*. We all want to be treated with kindness and respect, right?

Focus on getting to know the person, just like how you would get to know anyone else. What is their name? What are their hobbies? Do they have pets? What is their favorite flavor of ice cream?

When I was in the fourth grade, I switched elementary schools. I had to meet a new teacher and new classmates. I wanted to make new friends. Plus, I had to **navigate** a new environment in my wheelchair. I was nervous!

Everything turned out okay because people got to know *me*, and not just my disability. The best way people got to know me and I got to know them was by simply asking each other our names, where we grew up, and what our favorite hobbies were. I love to play video games, watch movies, and eat ice cream. See! People with disabilities are just like everyone else.

What are some things you love?

It's nice to offer your help before stepping in.

ASK FIRST, DON'T ASSUME

Wanting to help other people is an excellent quality to have. However, do not assume that people with disabilities need help doing everything.

People with disabilities have a certain system or way of doing things. Our systems make it easy for us. Unwelcome help can end up making things more difficult, take longer, and make us feel uncomfortable or unsafe. Always be sure to first ask if your help is needed.

For example, I enjoy pushing myself in my wheelchair. Sometimes, other people assume I need help and push me without asking. I do not like this. This makes me feel unsafe and out of control of my wheelchair and my body.

Do not touch someone's **mobility** or **accessibility device** without asking first. You should always keep your hands to yourself when interacting with anyone, and that includes their personal items.

Mobility and accessibility devices, like wheelchairs or hearing aids, are very personal. They are

Make a Guess!

Let's practice offering our help to others. Here are some examples below. Can you think of any other ways to *ask first*?

- Is there anything I can do to help you?
- Can I assist you with that?
- Do you need help pushing your wheelchair?
- How can I help?

extensions of our bodies. These devices must always be treated with respect and care. They should be handled only by their operator unless special permission is granted.

People with disabilities are strong and independent. We know our abilities better than anyone else. If your help is not needed, respect that. If your help is accepted, be sure to listen to instructions and follow through!

THINK BEFORE YOU SPEAK

Chances are that you know someone who has a disability. You might have questions, be curious, and want to help. Those feelings are normal. However, it is important to think before you speak.

People with disabilities do not have to answer personal questions about their disability. Nobody likes to be asked rude, embarrassing, or very personal questions—especially in front of other people. Remember, treat people the way you want to be treated.

What are some things you love?

You still might have questions to help you understand how you can be a better friend to someone with a disability. That is okay! Here are tips on when to ask questions:

- Do ask during personal one-on-one time, like a hangout session or a close conversation.
- Don't ask in front of large groups of people. No one wants an audience!

Ask Questions!

How would you feel being asked a personal question in front of a group of people? Think about how this might make someone else feel.

RESPECT AND DIGNITY

Remember, people with disabilities are like everyone else. We want to be seen as individuals that are **valued** members of the community.

Chances are that you or someone you know has a disability. If you are unsure, now you can say you know me! Now you have the tools to be mindful, **inclusive**, and respectful to the disabled community and beyond.

Look!

Take a look around! Is your environment accessible to people with disabilities? Ask someone with a disability how things can be made more accessible. Make a list and get to work!

EXTEND YOUR LEARNING

Did you know that December 3 is International Day of Persons with Disabilities? This day was created by the **United Nations** in 1992. Its goal is to promote understanding of disability issues and to mobilize support, **dignity**, and dedication to upholding **human rights** for the disabled community around the world. Learn more and get involved at www.idpwd.org.

GLOSSARY

accessibility device (ik-seh-suh-BIHL-uh-tee dih-VYS) equipment or software that helps people with disabilities live and work, including braille displays, hearing aids, and screen magnifiers

activist (AK-tih-vist) a person who fights for equality, inclusion, and human rights

dignity (DIG-nuh-tee) the state of quality of being worthy of honor and respect

human rights (HYOO-muhn RYTZ) rights that belong to all human beings, including the right to life, freedom, and dignity

inclusive (in-KLOO-siv) having a goal to include as many different types of people as possible

manual (MAN-yoo-uhl) done with the hands

minority (muh-NOHR-uh-tee) a group of people who are different from the larger population

mobility device (moh-BIH-luh-tee dih-VYS) equipment designed to help people with disabilities move, including wheelchairs, walkers, canes, and crutches

navigate (NAV-uh-gayt) to find a way through

osteogenesis imperfecta (ah-stee-uh-JEH-nuh-suhs im-puhr-FEK-tuh) a disability characterized by extreme fragility of bones; people with this disability may have many broken bones

United Nations (yoo-NYE-tuhd) an organization of many nations started in 1945 to promote world peace and understanding

valued (VAL-yood) something or someone who is worthy and important

FIND OUT MORE

Books

Burcaw, Shane. *Not So Different: What You Really Want to Ask about Having a Disability.* New York, NY: Roaring Books Press, 2017.

Burnell, Cerrie. *I Am Not a Label: 34 Disabled Artists, Thinkers, Athletes and Activists From Past and Present.* London, UK: Wide Eyed Editions, 2020.

Websites

Get Involved with Easterseals
https://www.easterseals.com/get-involved
Learn about the different ways you can get involved in increasing opportunities for people with disabilities, from advocacy to volunteering.

YouTube—Disability Etiquette
https://www.youtube.com/watch?v=iG3pQp6HoQM
Learn respectful ways to interact with people with disabilities.

INDEX

ABOUT THE AUTHOR

Nicole Evans is an actress, writer, and disability rights and inclusion activist. She enjoys helping children with disabilities explore their identity and realize their full potential. Born with osteogenesis imperfecta, Nicole is a full-time wheelchair user. Nicole lives in Los Angeles, California.